It's Your Health!

Exercise

BEVERLEY GOODGER

W
FRANKLIN WATTS
LONDON•SYDNEY

First published in 2004 by Franklin Watts
96 Leonard Street, London EC2A 4XD

Franklin Watts Australia
45-51 Huntley Street
Alexandria, NSW 2015

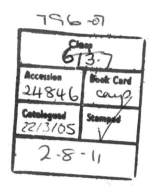

Series editor: Sarah Peutrill
Editor: Sarah Ridley
Designed by: Pewter Design Associates
Series design: Peter Scoulding
Illustration: Michael Courtney, Mike Saunders, Guy Smith, Roger Stewart
Picture researcher: Sophie Hartley
Series consultant: Wendy Anthony, Health Education Unit, Education
Service, Birmingham City Council
Picture credits: Action Images: 27. Samuel Ashfield/Science Photo
Library: 5. © Bettmann/Corbis: 9. Photo from www.JohnBirdsall.co.uk: 8.
© J. de Bounevialle/Photofusion: 13t. © Jacky Chapman/Photofusion: 24.
Dr Ray Clark & Mervyn Goff/Science Photo Library: 32. Digital
Vision/Robert Harding: 35. Chad Ehlers/Alamy: 28. Chris Fairclough: 12,
13b, 14, 17, 29, 39. David Gregs/Alamy: 10. Gusto/Science Photo
Library: 31t. ImageState/Alamy: 11. © David Katzenberger/Corbis: 38. ©
Ute Klaphake/Photofusion: 4, 40, 45. © Julie Lemberger/Corbis: 18. ©
Ulrike Preuss/Photofusion: 33. © Roger Ressmeyer/Corbis: 37. Françoise
Sauze/Science Photo Library: 19t. Thinkstock/Alamy: 23. © Frank
Trapper/Corbis: 25. © E.H. Wallop/Corbis: 41. © Franklin Watts
Publishers: 21, 30, 31b. © Catherine Wessel/Corbis: 19b.

The Publisher would like to thank the Brunswick Club for Young People,
Fulham, London for their help with this book. Thanks to our models,
including Stevie Waite.

A CIP catalogue record for this book is available from the British Library

ISBN 0 7496 5573 9

Printed in Malaysia

Contents

What is exercise?

There are many different meanings for the word 'exercise', but they all involve making an effort (exertion) for the sake of training or improvement. Physical exercise involves using our muscles to improve the way our bodies work. Together with a balanced diet, regular exercise increases physical fitness, improves health, and even lifts the spirits.

As well as improving muscle and bone strength, activities like climbing create a sense of pride in our achievements.

Regular exercise

Children between the ages of 5 and 18 should take part in at least one hour of moderate physical activity each day. Brisk walking, swimming and dancing are enjoyable activities that help to keep the heart and lungs working effectively.

Activities that involve climbing, gymnastics and skipping movements help to strengthen muscles and bones and keep joints supple.

Opportunities for exercise

We don't only have to exercise by changing into our gym gear! Throughout the day there are many opportunites to get moving - we can walk to school or the shops, or take the stairs instead of a lift. If we like to watch the TV, we can do a few exercises during the advertisements - it's amazing how many exercises we can fit in!

Past and present

In the past, children led active lifestyles. They played outside a lot, rode their bikes, walked to school and around their neighbourhood. In the UK, the average number of kilometres walked each year by children aged 11 to 15 has dropped by almost 200 kilometres since 1985. In the USA 25 per cent of children watch more than four hours of TV every day - which reduces the time that they can spend on being active.

It's your opinion

Some people choose to go to school or work in a car rather than walk even a short distance. What do you think prevents them from walking? What could be done to change this habit?

It's your decision

Can you make changes that make you more active?
Examine your day and work out when you can be more active - for example:
Could you walk or cycle to school?
Could you volunteer to walk someone's dog?

In the 1930s, games in the street were a part of everyday life for many children, such as here in New York, USA.

Why should we exercise?

Exercise is good for our health. Physical exercise improves our fitness, increasing stamina, suppleness and strength. Being fit makes the body able to fight disease and improves our quality of life right into old age. Exercise also helps us to relax and sleep well.

▼ Gymnastics helps to develop suppleness and strength.

Stamina
Stamina, or endurance, helps us to keep going. Activities such as gentle jogging and 'step' exercises provide good stamina-building exercise. They help to strengthen the heart and allow us to breathe more effectively.

Suppleness
Suppleness, or flexibility, allows us to bend and move easily. It improves the way we stand and our co-ordination, and helps to prevent injuries such as sprains and torn muscles.

Strength
Strength allows our muscles and bones to work effectively. Strong muscles are well-toned, improving the way we stand (posture) and helping to prevent injuries.

It's your decision

Is one form of exercise enough? Each activity has a different effect on your physical fitness. Some, like skipping, will benefit the body's strength and suppleness but have little effect on its flexibility. Swimming is a good all-round activity for your whole body.

▲ Participating in sports can give everyone that 'feel good' factor.

Uplifting exercise

Physical fitness also affects our mood. As well as being very enjoyable, vigorous exercise can cause the brain to release chemicals, called endorphins, into the blood stream. These produce a feeling of exhilaration. We feel proud of our physical improvement, and this increases our self-esteem.

It's your experience

'I love sport. It makes me feel happy and full of energy. I love running round in the fresh air.'

Elizabeth, aged 11

What do your favourite exercises do for you?

Exercise	Stamina	Suppleness	Strength
Badminton	beneficial effects	very good	beneficial effects
Baseball	beneficial effects	little effect	beneficial effects
Basketball	very good	beneficial effects	very good
Cycling	excellent	beneficial effects	beneficial effects
Dancing (fast)	very good	excellent	beneficial effects
Football	very good	beneficial effects	very good
Gymnastics	beneficial effects	excellent	very good
Jogging	excellent	beneficial effects	beneficial effects
Judo	beneficial effects	very good	beneficial effects
Rollerblading	very good	little effect	beneficial effects
Skipping (fast)	excellent	little effect	beneficial effects
Swimming	excellent	excellent	excellent
Tennis	beneficial effects	very good	beneficial effects
Walking	beneficial effects	little effect	little effect

Key:

✗	beneficial effects	very good	excellent
little effect	beneficial effects	very good	excellent

Stamina

Stamina allows you to exercise for longer without getting tired. The official title for stamina-building exercise is 'cardio-respiratory fitness'. When carried out regularly, it increases the strength of the heart muscle ('cardio' refers to the heart) and also lung capacity (how deeply we can breathe in and out).

Stamina-building exercise

There are two types of stamina-building exercise: aerobic and anaerobic exercise.

Aerobic exercise is carried out at a steady pace. By using the skeletal muscles (the ones that move your skeleton) at a steady pace, aerobic exercise slowly increases the body's demand for oxygen.

Examples of aerobic exercise include brisk walking, skipping, swimming, cycling and step-aerobics. To stay fit, we need 20 minutes of aerobic exercise, three times each week.

Skipping is an excellent way to improve stamina.

It's your opinion

Why do you think people choose not to exercise, even though it will improve their health? What puts people off? Do you think the government should do more to encourage people to exercise?

Anaerobic exercise is carried out in short bursts, making muscle cells work so hard that they use up all the oxygen available to them. Sprinting is a good example. We need to breathe deeply afterwards to replace the oxygen. Three 20-minute sessions of anaerobic exercise a week will help to keep us fit. See pages 34-35 for more on these kinds of exercise.

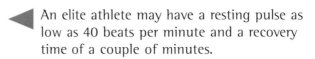

An elite athlete may have a resting pulse as low as 40 beats per minute and a recovery time of a couple of minutes.

Changes in pulse rate with exercise

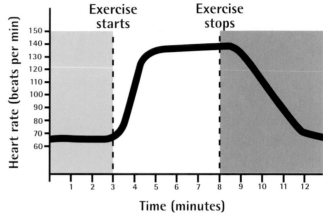

Pulse rate

Blood is carried away from the heart in arteries, whose thick muscular walls are stretched and then spring back into shape after each high pressure surge of blood from the heart. Each pulse is the result of one heart beat, felt as a pulse or throb in your arteries.

During stamina-building exercise, our pulse rate should be pushed up, or we won't strengthen our heart muscles. However, we should not work too hard, or we'll get too tired to keep going!

As we take more regular exercise we may find that our resting pulse and recovery time decrease.

Use the tips of the fingers on one hand to find your wrist pulse: it is under the skin, just below the thumb joint. Using a stop watch, count the number of pulse beats in 60 seconds. This will give you your resting pulse. Now carry out a minute of vigorous exercise. Measure your pulse rate again. It will be higher. How long does it take to return to the first measurement? The amount of time it takes for your pulse rate to return to its resting rate is called the recovery time. The faster a person's recovery time, the fitter they are.

It's your experience

'I think it is easier for the boys to keep fit than the girls. I like running around at lunchtime but my friends only want to stand and chat. The sports' teacher is going to run aerobics classes at lunchtime next term. I'm going to go twice a week.'

Kirstie, aged 12

The heart

The heart is the muscular organ that pumps blood around the body. The blood supplies the cells of the body with the food, oxygen and other chemicals they need to keep working, and carries away their waste products.

Heart beat

The human heart beats about 70 times a minute without stopping. That's over 100,000 times a day, forcing the body's five litres of blood through more than 80,000 kilometres of arteries, veins and capillaries. Unlike the skeletal muscles that help us to move, we have no voluntary control over the heart (cardiac) muscle, which never tires.

◀ The fist shows the position of the heart. It lies between the lungs, protected by the breast bone (sternum) and the ribs.

Oxygen-poor blood enters the heart from the upper body

Blood filled with oxygen is pumped out to supply the body

Deoxygenated blood is pumped out to the lungs, where the blood is oxygenated

Blood filled with oxygen enters the heart

Oxygen-poor blood enters the heart from the lower body

▲ In humans, blood passes through the heart twice in one complete circuit round the body. It's important to keep your heart healthy so that it pumps blood around the body efficiently.

It's your experience

'I swim at a club twice a week. Sometimes we work on technique and speed, but often we build up our stamina and improve our strokes by swimming up and down the pool for the whole session. I used to get really tired at first, but now I think I'm fitter and stronger than I was before I started'.
Mark, aged 13

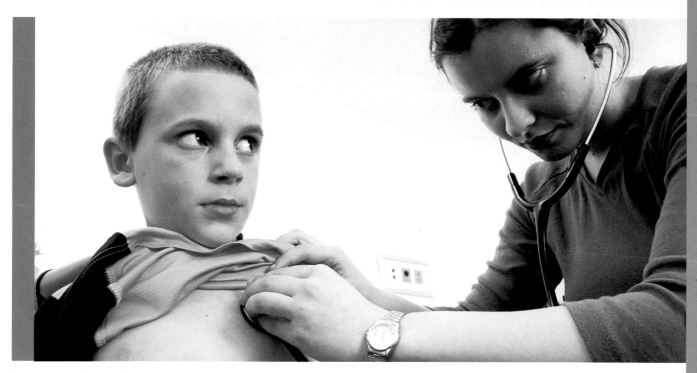

Increasing heart strength

Stamina-building exercise increases the strength of the heart muscle and helps to prevent the build-up of fatty deposits in the walls of the arteries (see pages 36–37).

By making the heart contract more efficiently a greater volume of blood is squeezed through the heart and into the arteries with each beat. The amount of blood per heart beat is called the 'stroke volume'.

Resting pulse

If we take part in regular sessions of stamina-building exercise, we may find that although our pulse rate increases rapidly during and just after exercise, our resting pulse may be lower than that of someone who doesn't exercise much. This is because a heart with a large stroke volume uses fewer contractions to circulate the same volume of blood as a heart with a smaller stroke volume.

You can hear a person's heartbeat by listening to it with a stethoscope.

Stroke volume is also important in returning blood to the heart through the veins. When the chambers of the heart relax between contractions, blood is 'sucked' into the heart from the veins. A heart with a large stroke volume will draw a greater volume of blood back into the heart from the veins with each heart beat than one with a smaller stroke volume.

It's your decision

Are you looking after your future health? The American Heart Foundation website states that: 'Inactive children, when compared with active children, weigh more, have higher blood pressure and lower levels of heart-protective high-density lipoproteins.' These all increase the risk of developing coronary heart disease in later life.

The lungs

Like the heart, the lungs work automatically. They are the body's breathing machine, providing our cells with the oxygen they need to produce energy. The lungs also breathe out the waste carbon dioxide from these cells.

Lung capacity

Stamina-building exercise makes us breathe faster and harder than we do when we are resting. This exercises and strengthens the diaphragm and intercostal muscles which are responsible for the expansion and contraction of the chest cavity as we breathe.

If we have strong breathing movements, we will have a large lung capacity, and will be able to swap large volumes of used and fresh air with each breath.

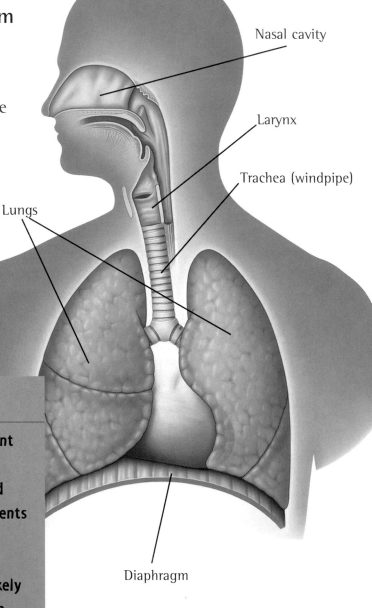

Nasal cavity

Larynx

Trachea (windpipe)

Lungs

Diaphragm

Air enters through the nose or mouth and passes through tubes into the lungs where oxygen is removed.

It's your opinion

Because playing sport increases the amount of air we breathe in, polluted air can be a problem. In a US study children who played three or more outdoor sports in environments with high levels of ozone pollution (which comes from the exhaust fumes of motor vehicles) were more than three times as likely to develop asthma compared with children who did not play any sports. There was no increased risk where the air was clean. What should be done?

Out of breath

Even when we are resting, our intercostal and diaphragm muscles are stimulated to contract and relax by nerve impulses from the brain. The amount of carbon dioxide in the blood provides the brain with information about the energy demands of the cells.

Air in

Air out

When resting, we breathe in and out about 15 times each minute. Each breath contains about half a litre of air.

Ribs (the intercostal muscles are attached to the ribs and make them move in and out)

Diaphragm

Breathing in (the diaphragm flattens and the rib cage moves out and up, making the chest cavity bigger)

Breathing out (the rib cage moves down and in and the diaphragm returns to its relaxed domed shape)

If energy demand increases, as it does during exercise, so will the amount of carbon dioxide in the blood. The result is that the brain sends nerve impulses to the intercostal muscles and the diaphragm more rapidly than when we are resting, and this increases the rate and depth of breathing. In the meantime, we can feel out of breath until enough oxygen gets through to our cells and the levels of carbon dioxide in the blood drop back to 'normal'.

It's your decision

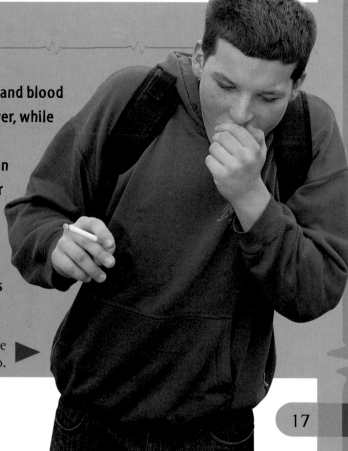

Does smoking affect your performance?
When we smoke, the nicotine increases heart rate and blood pressure and can cause arteries to become narrower, while the carbon monoxide we inhale with the cigarette smoke reduces the amount of oxygen our blood can carry. This means that when smokers exercise their heart has to beat very quickly and they have to breathe very hard to supply the cells of their bodies with the oxygen they need. They will tire more quickly and become more breathless than non-smokers.

Smokers pay much more than the price of the cigarettes for their habit – it affects their health too.

Suppleness

Suppleness means how flexible your body is – how easily you can bend and stretch. If you are supple, you will be able to make a wide range of movements using your muscles and joints. If you lack suppleness, then you are likely to suffer sprain, strain and tear injuries when you try to exercise.

It's your experience

'Last term we were all involved in dance workshops with professional dancers. They performed a routine for us at the beginning of the week and they were amazing – so flexible and fit. I really enjoyed the workshops that followed and now I belong to a dance group. I can already feel that I have better control of my body'.

Jo, aged 13

Ballet dancers are superb athletes. Their ballet training develops their suppleness, stamina and strength to a level that makes their graceful movements appear totally effortless.

It's your decision

Are you satisfied with your flexibility? Many people can't touch their toes and don't believe it's important. How flexible do you need to be?

Would you like to be as supple as this? ▶

Achieving suppleness

Suppleness is developed through gentle stretching, and should be part of your warm up/warm down routine (see pages 40-41). Activities such as yoga, swimming, dancing and gymnastics all develop suppleness.

It is recommended that teenagers carry out exercises that develop suppleness at least three times a week.

Flexibility is joint-specific, which means that if your knee joints are flexible, it does not follow that your shoulder joints are. For this reason, exercises that develop suppleness should work on a range of joints.

How supple are you?

You can get an idea of your suppleness from this simple test. Sit on the floor with your legs straight out in front of you and reach towards your toes. If you can reach beyond your toes you are very supple. If you can just reach your toes you are average and if you can just reach your ankles or shins you have poor suppleness.

▼ Flexibility is important for all types of sport, but it is also important in everyday life. It's not only footballers who need to be able to bend down to tie their laces!

Joints

Movements of the human body are brought about by skeletal muscles pulling on bones. A place where two bones meet is called a joint. Some joints, like those in the skull, don't move, and are called fixed joints, but most joints in the body are movable, and play a part in making us flexible.

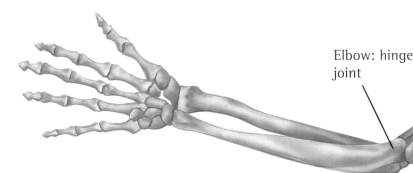

Elbow: hinge joint

Shoulder: ball and socket joint

Keeping joints healthy helps us to move freely. Even simple actions such as bending our arms depend on the joint.

Ligaments and tendons
Bones are held together at the joints by tough, elastic ligaments. Skeletal muscles are attached to the bones that they pull on by tough, inelastic bands of connective tissue, called tendons.

When we bend and stretch our bodies, we rely on the elasticity of the muscles to allow us to do it. If we aren't supple enough, or if we bend a joint in the wrong direction, then the tendons and ligaments will cause the muscle to tear (see page 25), or will be torn or stretched themselves. This will produce a painful sprain, strain or tear.

Sometimes, the damage is so severe that the joint permanently loses some or all of its flexibility. This is why it is so important to warm up and gently stretch your muscles before participating in any physical activity.

The knee joint is a hinge joint because it only allows movement backwards and forwards.

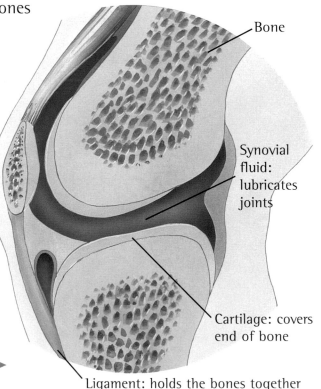

Bone

Synovial fluid: lubricates joints

Cartilage: covers end of bone

Ligament: holds the bones together

It's your experience

'Last year I sprained my ankle playing tennis. I thought it was better, but when I played tennis again a few weeks later, I went over on it again. After that, I did lots of exercises to strengthen the muscles in my ankle, and it seems better, but I still wear ankle strapping when I play tennis!'

Bev, aged 17

It's your decision

Are you worried about something that won't become a problem until old age?
Children whose diets are rich in calcium, and who take plenty of weight-bearing exercise will develop strong, healthy skeletons that will support them all their lives. Children who have little calcium in their diet and who take little exercise are likely to develop weak skeletons. Weak skeletons are easily damaged in old age.

Looking after your joints

Flexible muscles and smoothly working joints ensure that your posture (body position) is good, and that all the parts of your body are held in the right place.

Today, many people are living long lives so their bodies need to be kept in working order for longer. Hip and knee joints take a great deal of strain when we walk and run, and replacement operations for these joints are now commonplace.

Regular, moderate exercise that retains the flexibility of these joints, and strengthens the muscles around them, will help to keep them healthy for longer, as will a diet that contains calcium-rich foods.

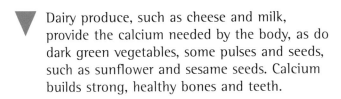 Dairy produce, such as cheese and milk, provide the calcium needed by the body, as do dark green vegetables, some pulses and seeds, such as sunflower and sesame seeds. Calcium builds strong, healthy bones and teeth.

Muscles

Our bodies contain 640 skeletal muscles. They are arranged into groups that work as teams to move different parts. Skeletal muscles are voluntary, meaning we control the movements they bring by sending instructions from our brain.

Pull, not push

Skeletal muscles can only contract (pull) and relax. When the biceps muscle, at the front of the upper arm, contracts, your arm bends. To straighten your arm again, the triceps muscle at the back of the upper arm has to contract, while the biceps relaxes.

The structure of skeletal muscle

Skeletal muscles are composed of long, rod-shaped cells called muscle fibres, which can be up to 30 centimetres long. Each muscle fibre is made of thousands of thinner strands called myofibrils. These contain two types of interlocking protein myofilaments; thick myosin filaments and thin actin filaments.

Skeletal muscles are called striated muscles because of the stripy appearance that these alternating actin and myosin filaments give the muscle fibres.

The voluntary skeletal muscles at the front of the body.

Running through each skeletal muscle are hundreds of thousands of long, thin muscle fibres.

Fasicle (bundle of muscle fibres)

Whole skeletal muscle (rod-shaped cells)

Myofibril

Actin filament

Myosin filament

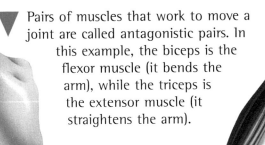

Pairs of muscles that work to move a joint are called antagonistic pairs. In this example, the biceps is the flexor muscle (it bends the arm), while the triceps is the extensor muscle (it straightens the arm).

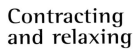

Biceps muscle

Triceps muscle

Contracting and relaxing

When a muscle contracts, the actin filaments slide over the myosin filaments, making the muscles shorter and fatter. When the muscle relaxes, the muscle returns to its resting length.

Muscles and exercise

Exercising improves muscular fitness and strength: it makes us stronger, so we are able to do more things. This happens especially when we do exercises that put our muscles under stress, for example when we lift weights. When muscles recover from this stress their fibres get bigger and this makes them stronger and more powerful.

Some people exercise to increase the size of their muscles, simply because they think it improves their looks. While the big, strong muscles that strength training produces may look impressive, they are only capable of short-lived, explosive bursts of power.

It's your opinion

Athletes sometimes hit the news because they have tested positive for performance-enhancing drugs, including anabolic steroids that build up the muscles. What makes these athletes risk their sporting careers?

Strength

A strong body is a well-supported body, helping us to stand properly and reducing the risk of injury. Our personal strength can be shown in how much force a muscle or a group of muscles can produce in a sudden burst, like a hard push or pull, or over a period of time. The stronger our muscles, the better we are at producing both types of force.

Swimming is an excellent activity for building muscle strength.

Using your muscles

The more we use our muscles the healthier and stronger they become. When we use a muscle to lift, push or pull things, it makes that muscle get larger (this is called hypertrophy). If you do not use a muscle at all, it begins to get smaller and weaker (called atrophy).

It's your experience

'When I broke a bone in my elbow, I was in a plaster cast for six weeks. It was weird when they took the plaster cast off. My arm looked really thin, and felt very weak. It took a couple of days before it felt like it was my arm again, and a few weeks before the muscles in my arm looked normal to me!'

Jack, aged 13

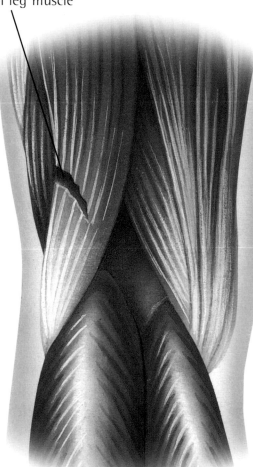

Torn leg muscle

Strong muscles

Strong muscles pulling hard on the bones to produce strong movements help to strengthen the bones, making them less likely to break. They also give good support to your joints, reducing the risk of injury by 'taking the strain'. Activities such as rowing, digging in the garden, cycling or swimming can increase the strength of your skeletal muscles and your bones.

Muscle problems

Stressed muscles must be rested. When we carry out a lot of muscle-building activity, such as lifting, pulling or pushing, our muscles are put under stress. It is important to rest our muscles if they have been stressed, as this recovery period gives them time to get bigger and more powerful. Remember that lifting, pulling and pushing too forcefully can damage our muscles.

◄ Sudden movements during exercise can cause a muscle to tear. The muscle has to be rested so that it can heal itself.

It's your opinion

Well-toned muscles produce a trim body shape. While most people agree that strong muscles are important for health and fitness, is there too much pressure on young people to have the perfect body? What problems might this lead to?

Research has shown that TV programmes featuring slim and beautiful people make viewers dissatisfied with their ► own appearance, while those that don't have anything to do with personal appearance don't have any effect on how attractive they think they are. Generally, however, both men and women who participate in sport have a more positive body-image than those who do not, and are affected less by what's on their TV.

The immune system

Our immune system is responsible for helping us to fight infections caused by bacteria and viruses. Research suggests that light to moderate exercise, where we feel slightly warm and are a little out of breath, helps our immune system to work well.

When to exercise

Our bodies have a daily rhythm of activity, sometimes called the body clock, and recent studies have indicated that our immune system is least effective at fighting infection early in the morning. This means that we are most at risk of being infected by bacteria and viruses at this time.

The heavy training sessions that world class athletes perform often early in the morning, increase a chemical in the blood that is known to suppress the immune system. For them the best time to train may be around six pm – the time of day when the human immune system is at its peak. For most people, however, light exercise at any time of day may actually help our immune systems to work effectively.

When we're not feeling well

Although exercise is good for us, it is probably best not to carry out strenuous exercise if we have a heavy cold or are unwell. We won't feel much like exercising if we are tired, if our muscles and joints ache or feel stiff or if we can't breathe because of a blocked nose. Resting for a day or two will give our immune system time and energy to get on with the job of fighting the infection. When our immune system has destroyed the invading viruses or bacteria, we will begin to feel better and more energetic, and then we can begin to exercise again.

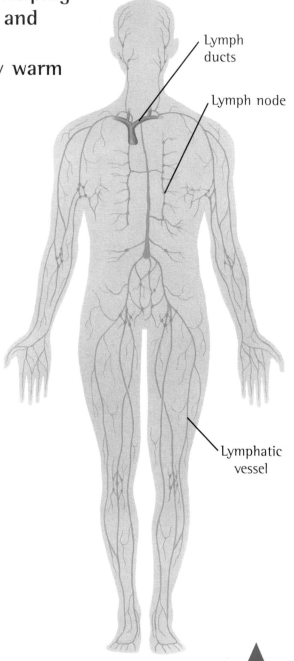

Lymph ducts

Lymph node

Lymphatic vessel

The lymphatic system reaches all parts of the body. This system plays a vital role in protecting the body against infection. Many of the vessels pass through muscles which help to squeeze lymph – watery fluid – around the body.

It's your decision

Would you exercise when you are ill? It's sometimes best to rest, and not exercise, when we are feeling unwell. However, some people prefer to exercise anyway, feeling that they don't want to let illness dictate their life.

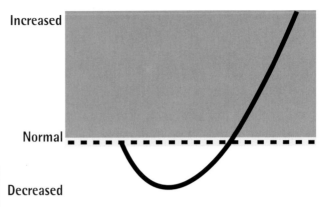

Risk of infection compared with amount of training

Risk of infection — Increased / Normal / Decreased

Amount of exercise — Sedentary / Moderate / Very high

Too much exercise?

Sometimes too much exercise can work against the immune system. Very strenuous exercise, with little recovery time between sessions, seems to prevent it from working efficiently. Endurance athletes, such as marathon runners, are more likely to develop a cold during the week after an endurance event than at other, less demanding times in their training schedule.

▲ Marathon running is a very strenuous activity. The risk of catching an infection is increased immediately after a marathon race.

It's your experience

'Exercise makes me feel good, but I don't know whether it helps to stop me from catching colds. I think that playing sport when I've got a bit of a cold helps me to stop thinking about it, so I feel better than I would if I was sitting at home feeling sorry for myself.'

Mike, aged 14

Mood

Exercise is a good way to improve our mood. It can provide our minds with a positive focus, it helps to improve concentration, brainpower and physical co-ordination, and can boost our self-esteem. Exercise can also develop our social skills by helping us to make friends.

Finding an exercise activity that suits your needs, lifestyle and enjoyment will help you to meet people like yourself. ▼

Endorphins

Some forms of strenuous exercise may make you feel exhilarated because they stimulate the pituitary gland in the brain to release chemicals called endorphins. Apart from making you feel good, endorphins also block nerve impulses that are carrying information to the brain about pain.

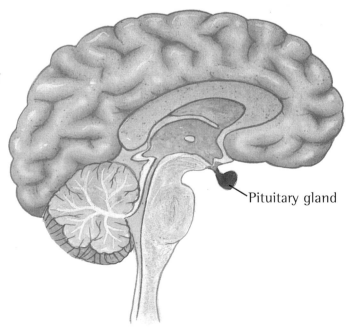

Pituitary gland

▶ The pituitary gland is situated at the base of the brain, immediately above the roof of the mouth.

Exercise addicts

These natural 'feel-good' body chemicals are similar in effect to opium-based drugs, such as heroin and morphine. The surge in endorphins experienced after vigorous exercise helps to explain why some people seem to become addicted to exercise. Just as drug addicts become totally dependent on increasingly large doses of drugs, an 'exercise addict' becomes dependent on daily, strenuous exercise to produce the endorphins they need to help them improve their mood.

Of course, a person can become addicted to exercise for other reasons. They may depend on it to escape from everyday pressures and anxieties, or they may use it to burn calories and keep themselves ultra slim because they are obsessed with their appearance.

While a daily workout has many health benefits, exercise addicts can seriously damage their bodies because they ignore illness, injury and the nutritional needs of their bodies.

It's your decision

Would you rather get the feel-good release of endorphins some other way?
Other activities have been found to release endorphins without the need to exercise. They include acupuncture (an ancient Chinese treatment for the relief of stress and pain), massage (a widely used technique that uses gentle pressure on the skin, muscles and joints to help relax the muscles and relieve stress) and eating chocolate (a very enjoyable but sometimes addictive activity).

It's your experience

'I put on some weight during my teens and after comments from some people I decided I had to lose it. I started exercising three times a week, but when I started to lose weight and feel pleased with the results I exercised more and more. I was exercising for two or three hours every day, and didn't have a social life, before I realised I had become obsessed with exercise and my appearance.'

Sarah, aged 21

Chocaholics may be addicted to the endorphins released by their pituitary gland when they eat chocolate.

Exercise and food

Exercise alone cannot make you physically fit. You must also supply your one hundred trillion (100,000,000,000,000) body cells with all the raw materials they need to work effectively. These raw materials are provided by the food that you eat.

A balanced diet will contain the correct amounts of different food types. The pyramid shows the proportions of each food type we should try to eat each day. This will ensure we can exercise at our optimum level. ▼

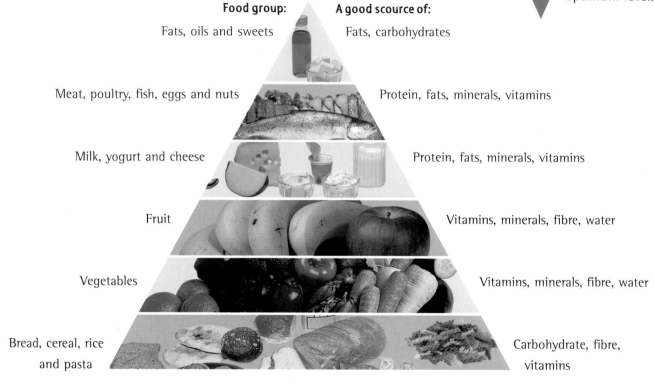

Food group:		A good scource of:
Fats, oils and sweets		Fats, carbohydrates
Meat, poultry, fish, eggs and nuts		Protein, fats, minerals, vitamins
Milk, yogurt and cheese		Protein, fats, minerals, vitamins
Fruit		Vitamins, minerals, fibre, water
Vegetables		Vitamins, minerals, fibre, water
Bread, cereal, rice and pasta		Carbohydrate, fibre, vitamins

It's your opinion

Exercise can reduce the risk of becoming overweight, but on its own it is not enough. Some people eat a lot of fatty or sugary foods, making it all too easy to consume more raw materials than they use up with exercise. With more people becoming overweight, which do you think is to blame – lack of exercise or a poor diet?

Too much or too little

To stay healthy, we must eat enough of the right foods to supply the needs of our cells. Eat too little, and our cells will run short of raw materials, and may stop working properly. Eat too much, and we may have to store the raw materials until they are needed. If we eat a balanced diet, then our body can supply the raw materials that our cells depend on, whenever they are needed.

Fuel up

When we exercise we need to make sure that our bodies have the right fuel. To avoid being too hungry or too full it is best to eat a meal about three hours before we exercise. Carbohydrate-rich foods such as bread and pasta are best, as foods high in fat take longer to digest. If you need a snack, eat it 30 minutes before and choose something like a piece of fruit or a cereal bar.

During exercise the body burns off a lot of carbohydrate so these stores need to be replaced when we finish exercising. This means we should eat a carbohyrate food or drink after exercising, especially if we exercise every day.

To be healthy you need to eat the right foods, as well as exercise. Crisps are a popular snack but are high in fat. ▶

What is in your favourite snack?

	Ready salted crisps (100g)	Milk chocolate (100g)	Apple (100g)
Carbohydrate	50.7g	57.1g	11.8g
Protein	6.6g	7.8g	0.4g
Fat	35.1g	29.9g	0.1g

It's your decision

Do you leave time to digest your food before exercising?
After a meal, your stomach needs blood to help it digest your food, but when you exercise, your muscles need a good flow of blood to supply the contracting and relaxing muscle fibres with oxygen.

Don't forget water!

All the chemical reactions that take place in the body depend on water, and we should drink about six glasses each day to replace what we lose in our breath, through sweating and in our urine.

When we exercise, our bodies sweat more because sweating acts to cool down our hard-working bodies and keep them at the right temperature. We must replace this lost water, and this may mean drinking up to 20 glasses of water over 24 hours on a day when we are exercising hard.

Energy

Without a source of energy, the cells of the body will stop working. The energy is used by the cells to maintain the normal body functions which are needed to keep us alive. It allows the body to grow and repair itself and allows us to move. The carbohydrates, fats and proteins in the food we eat provide us with the energy that we need.

Metabolic rate

The rate at which a person converts food into energy is called their metabolic rate. It is measured when the person is at complete rest, and varies from person to person. People with a slow metabolic rate will convert food into energy more slowly and so will put on weight more easily. People with a fast metabolic rate will convert food into energy faster and also tend to have more energy. Regular exercise can help to raise our metabolic rate.

When the body uses energy, heat is produced. Exercise increases the rate at which the body uses energy, and so we feel hot. In this thermograph of a man on a bike, the muscles that are used to exercise look red and yellow because they are hot.

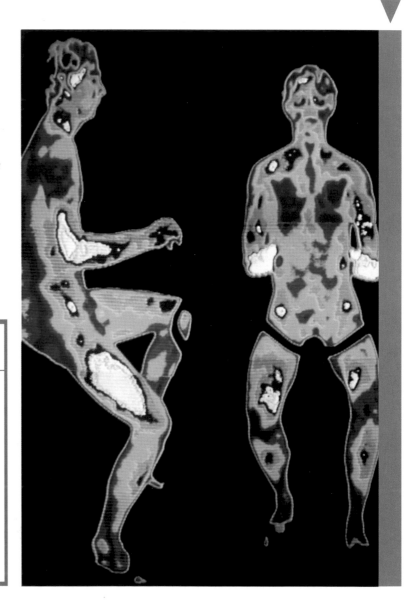

It's your experience

'It's so unfair. I only have to look at a chocolate bar and I put on weight, but my friend eats loads and is built like a stick insect. We both do about the same amount of sport, so I suppose she must just burn up her food faster than me'.
Claire, aged 15

Daily energy requirements

The total amount of energy needed by a person each day depends on how active and how heavy they are, with heavy, active people requiring the most. Boys and men tend to use more energy in a day than girls and women of a similar age. This is because males are usually heavier and more muscular than females of the same age.

Everyone needs different amounts of food, depending on how much energy their body uses.

Someone who takes a lot of exercise each day will require more energy-giving food than a person of the same age, weight and sex who doesn't take regular exercise.

Energy is measured in units called joules (J) and calories (cal). We use so much energy each day that these units are usually expressed as kilocalories (kcal) (one thousand calories), kilojoules (kJ) (one thousand joules), or even sometimes megajoules (MJ) (one million joules).

Estimated average requirements for energy (EAR) for children and adolescents MJ/day (kcal/day)		
	Boys	**Girls**
7–10 years	8.24 (1,970)	7.28 (1,740)
11–14 years	9.27 (2,220)	7.72 (1,845)
15–18 years	11.5 (2,755)	8.83 (2,110)

Releasing energy

The body releases energy from the food we eat through a series of chemical reactions called cell respiration. This takes place inside all our cells. There are two types of cell respiration: aerobic and anaerobic cell respiration.

Aerobic respiration

During aerobic cell respiration (respiration with oxygen), oxygen and glucose are carried to the respiring cells in the blood. Inside the cells, the oxygen is used to release the chemical energy that is stored in the glucose.

During aerobic exercise, the flow of oxygen-rich blood to the muscles must increase, and your body achieves this in several ways. First the heart rate increases. Then blood flow is diverted to the muscles from other organs. Oxygen is released from the blood efficiently and carbon dioxide is carried away to be breathed out through the lungs.

Inside a mitochondrion, aerobic respiration produces large amounts of a chemical called ATP (adenosine triphosphate), which acts as an energy store inside the cell.

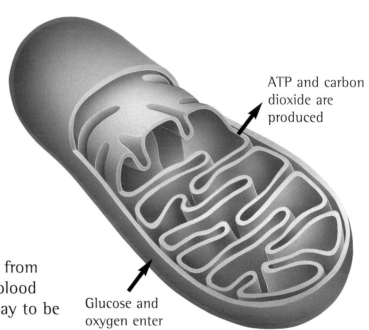

ATP and carbon dioxide are produced

Glucose and oxygen enter

It's your opinion

A study carried out in the USA in 2003 revealed that cardio-respiratory fitness (the type that is increased by aerobic exercise) in early adulthood significantly reduced the chance of developing high blood pressure and diabetes in middle age. If aerobic exercise early in life is so important for health in later years, why isn't one hour of physical activity made a compulsory part of the daily curriculum for all school children?

It's your experience

'When we run round the school field, the muscles in my legs feel really heavy at the end, and they're shaky for ages afterwards.'

Louise, aged 14

Anaerobic respiration

Sometimes cells produce energy without using oxygen. This is called anaerobic cell respiration, and it is not very efficient. However it is useful when the supply of oxygen to the cell can't keep up with the cell's energy demands.

A sprinter's muscle cells require large amounts of energy to produce the powerful muscle contractions that force them along the track. By the end of the race, the muscle cells are respiring anaerobically because oxygen cannot be supplied to them quickly enough.

Anaerobic exercise releases lactic acid in the muscles, which can produce cramps and a feeling of tiredness. Immediately afterwards, an increased rate and depth of breathing, together with an increased heart rate, ensure that the oxygen supply to the muscle cells can once more meet the energy demand, and the sprinter recovers.

▼ Even though a sprint only lasts for a few seconds, an oxygen debt builds up in the sprinter's muscles, which must be repaid by rapid, deep breathing (panting) as soon as the race is over.

Face the facts

If we don't exercise enough and eat a diet high in fat we run the risk of developing life-threatening diseases such as coronary heart disease and diabetes.

Fatty deposits can build up in the walls of our arteries, narrowing our blood vessels and interfering with blood supply to cells. Exercise helps to reduce the rate at which these fatty plaques form.

Carried in the blood

Lack of exercise, combined with a diet high in fat, will increase the amount of fatty substances, such as cholesterol, carried by the blood. These fatty substances are deposited in the walls of our arteries from childhood onwards, so the more fat we carry in our blood, the faster these fatty 'plaques' build up.

Fatty substances deposited in the walls of the artery

Coronary arteries

The heart is supplied with essential supplies through the coronary arteries – these help the heart's own muscles to pump.

Gradually fatty deposits may block or narrow fine branches of the coronary artery, damaging the heart. This is the cause of coronary heart disease, which claims the lives of more than seven million people around the world each year.

Coronary artery

Regular exercise, a healthy, balanced diet and avoiding smoking and excessive drinking will all help to reduce the risk of developing coronary heart disease and other serious diseases such as high blood pressure, cancer, diabetes and arthritis later in life.

Energy balance

If a person's diet provides them with more energy than they need, they will store the extra energy as fat. If they eat less-energy-containing food than they need, they will use up some of their energy stores. Exercise can help to keep a balance between the amount of energy that is eaten and the amount that is used.

Childhood obesity

Children who don't take regular exercise and who have a diet which is high in fat may become obese. Obese children are likely to become obese adults, increasing their risk of developing coronary heart disease.

Childhood obesity can also cause childhood health problems such as 'type II diabetes', high blood pressure, asthma and poor bone growth and sleeping patterns. In the UK and the USA the number of obese and overweight children has doubled, and in Australia tripled, since 1990.

Obesity in children is increasing in many parts of the developed world. Regular exercise and a healthy diet help to reduce weight, and prevent long-term damage to health.

Obese children are putting their health in such danger that some experts are now predicting that obese children may be outlived by their parents.

It's your opinion

Most adults are aware of the fact that an unhealthy diet combined with a lack of exercise is bad for their hearts. Should the government do any more to help them or is it their own decision? What measures could the government put in place?

It's your experience

'My dad used to eat a lot of fatty things. He had a heart-attack two years ago but luckily the doctors saved his life. He eats a healthy diet now, and has lost a lot of weight so I think he'll be okay.'

Laura, aged 13

Exercise each day

We only need to exercise for 60 minutes out of the 1,440 minutes in a day! Remember, to keep physically fit, we should be combining one hour of exercise each day with a balanced diet. This can be difficult to achieve, but by setting small, achievable goals each day we can increase our fitness.

With so many different kinds of physical activity available, we should all be able to find at least one that suits our needs.

It's your decision

Will you make excuses not to exercise? Everyone makes excuses not to exercise sometimes. Maybe because it's too hot or too cold. It may be that there is something they want to watch on TV. Sixty minutes is not a lot of time out of your day, but whether you decide to exercise is up to you.

Keep a diary

Make a diary, keeping a note of how much exercise you do each day for a week – include things like walking to school. Also write down what you've had to eat. Work out where and when you can make improvements.

Some fitness tips

1. If you can, walk to and from school each day, or to the local shops.

2. Try to be active during break and lunchtime at school – walk about, or join a lunchtime club which involves physical activity, such as football, hockey or table tennis.

3. Try a new sport such as martial arts, dancing, volleyball or trampolining. Your local leisure centre may offer classes, or your school may run clubs in some of these – why not go along and try them out?

4. Turn exercise into a treat! A trip to the ice rink or dry ski slope will be good fun, great exercise and you won't forget it in a hurry!

5. Try some active jobs to help at home – gardening, vacuuming the carpets, cleaning the windows all use energy. Offer to take the dog for a walk.

6. Look for healthier alternatives to junk food snacks. Eat fruit when you want a quick bite to eat, or try a slice of bread (preferably brown) – it's just as filling as a packet of crisps, but does not contain any fat (unless you spread butter or margarine on it). Ask your parents if they could help you out by buying fewer fatty snacks and convenience foods.

7. Eat five portions of different fruit and vegetables each day.

An hour a day may sound a lot, but it's great fun working out your own exercise schedule, and you'll be amazed at how easily you can fit it into your life.

It's your experience

'When I was at school, all the clubs and activities were free, so keeping fit was easy and didn't cost me anything. Now I've left school, I have to pay if I want to use the sports facilities anywhere. Still, I think it's worth it – it keeps me fit and I meet my friends at the gym.'

Kate, aged 18

Eating fresh fruit and vegetables helps to keep us fit, well and raring to go! Research has also shown that by eating at least five portions of different fruit and vegetables each day we can reduce the risk of developing certain diseases, such as cancer, later in life.

How to exercise

It doesn't matter whether we exercise in just one session, or if we split it up into lots of smaller chunks throughout the day. What does matter is that we exercise for long enough (one hour in total), hard enough (so that we feel warm and slightly out of breath) and often enough (every day!) to keep fit.

How to exercise

When we begin to exercise we should always:

- Build up our exercise programme gradually, especially if we aren't usually very active. If we have any medical conditions, such as asthma, we should check our ideas with a doctor first.
- Choose a time and place carefully – don't exercise after a heavy meal – and stay safe – avoid busy roads, uneven ground or lonely places.
- Warm up before exercising – this will prepare our muscles, heart and lungs for their work-out.
- Drink plenty of water before, during and after our physical activity – then we won't become dehydrated.
- Cool down when we've finished – this will help to keep us supple, and prevent stiffness from setting in the next day.
- Vary the exercises and enjoy it – to keep exercise interesting and so we won't get bored and give up! Variety will also ensure that we exercise a range of muscles.
- Keep ourselves and our kit clean – sweating is an essential and healthy part of taking exercise, but afterwards there is nothing nicer than changing out of our sweaty kit and having a refreshing shower, bath or wash.

Enjoy yourself. Above all else, exercise should be fun!

40

Ways of warming up

Warm-up exercises should be done slowly and smoothly.

- Begin with some gentle aerobic exercise, such as jogging, to warm up muscles and to prepare the heart and lungs for action.

- Then do some gentle neck stretching exercises, circle the arms and finally do some side bends. These movements will help to loosen the muscles which move our joints in the neck, shoulders and back. Try not to over-bend however!

- The hamstring, inner thigh quadriceps and calf muscles all need to be gently stretched to remove stiffness (see page 22) so that they can contract and relax fully while we exercise. If we don't stretch them gently, then any sudden movements that we make may tear them.

It's your experience

'I don't play an hour of sport every day, but I think I'm probably active for at least an hour each day. I walk to and from the bus stop, I play football with my friends at break and lunchtime and I walk miles (well, it seems like miles) round school, carrying a heavy bag. We have two lessons of games or PE each week, and I do an after-school sport club once a week. I ride my bike, or go hill-walking at the weekend, too. Mind you, I do enjoy sitting still, playing a computer game, especially when I'm worn out!'

James, aged 12

It's your decision

Can you stay active for life? Research has shown that people who take up exercise when they are middle-aged live longer than top athletes who suddenly stop being active in mid-life.

◀ Remember to ease into your stretches, as sudden pushes or pulls damage our muscles.

And finally...

When we've finished an exercise session, we must cool down. Cooling down is similar to warming up. A gentle jog should be followed by the stretching and bending routine used in the warm up. Then put on some warm clothes so that the body cools down slowly.

Glossary

Aerobic exercise a type of exercise that uses the skeletal muscles to slowly increase the body's demand for oxygen, such as brisk walking or jogging

Antagonistic pair a pair of muscles that work in opposition to move a joint. One contracts while the other relaxes

Balanced diet a diet that contains all the foods we need for a healthy body, in the right proportions

Calorie the energy needed to raise the temperature of 1 gram of water from 14.5 to 15.5°C. 1 calorie = 4.184 joules

Carbon dioxide the waste gas that is produced by cell respiration. It is carried from the cells to the lungs in the blood, and is then breathed out

Cell respiration the process by which the energy released from food is used to form ATP (a high energy substance that stores energy inside the cell until it is needed)

Diaphragm the sheet of muscle that separates the lung cavity (thorax) from the abdomen. Contraction of the diaphragm muscle and the intercostal muscles between the ribs increases the volume of the thorax and draws air into the lungs

Glucose a type of carbohydrate used as a source of energy by the body

Heart the muscular organ that pumps the blood around the body

Immune system the system that defends the body against disease

Joint a place where two bones meet

Ligament bands of elastic tissue that hold the bones together

Lung capacity the amount of air the lungs can hold

Muscle a type of body tissue that can contract and relax and therefore create movement within the body

Oxygen the gas that is used by the cells during aerobic respiration

Pulse the regular stretching of the walls of arteries as the heartbeat causes blood to surge through them

Recovery time the time taken for our pulse to return to its resting rate after vigorous exercise

Skeletal muscle muscles that pull on the bones of the skeleton to move the body. They are under the conscious control of the brain

Stamina the ability to perform a physical activity for a long period of time

Stretching the gentle extension and relaxation of the main muscle groups that must be carried out before and after exercise to prevent injury

Strength the amount of force skeletal muscles can produce

Stroke volume the volume of blood pumped through the heart per heartbeat

Suppleness the ability to move, bend and stretch the limbs and body without injury

Warm-up a series of gentle exercises that prepare our muscles, heart and lungs for their work-out

Further information

UK

Lifebytes
A website that gives young people aged 11–14 facts about health in a fun and interesting way.

www.lifebytes.gov.uk/extras/about.html

BBC Health, Kids health
Features lots of interactive games on mind and body matters.

www.bbc.co.uk/health/kids/

Sport England
This website includes information on Active Schools, links to Sports Governing Bodies and lists sports facilities in your area.

3rd Floor Victoria House
Bloomsbury Square
London WC1B 4SE
Tel: 020 7273 1500
Fax: 020 7383 5740

www.sportengland.org/
Email: info@sportengland.org

USA

Kid's Health Website
The most visited site providing approved health information about children.

www.kidshealth.org/

Healthfinder
A website with lots of information about ways to be healthy and have fun.

www.healthfinder.gov/kids/default.htm

How stuff works website
Go to the health stuff and then the fitness section of this site for loads of information on how exercise works.

www.howstuffworks.com

Australia

The Australian Sports Commission (ASC)
Funds sport in Australia, developing elite sporting excellence and increasing community participation.

Leverrier Cres Bruce ACT 2617
PO Box 176 Belconnen ACT 2616
Telephone: 02 6214 1111
Facsimile: 02 6251 2680

www.ausport.gov.au
email to: asc@ausport.gov.au

Healthy and Active
A website containing practical information for families, parents, teenagers, children and their carers on healthy eating, physical activity and exercise.

www.healthyandactive.health.gov.au/kids.htm

Index

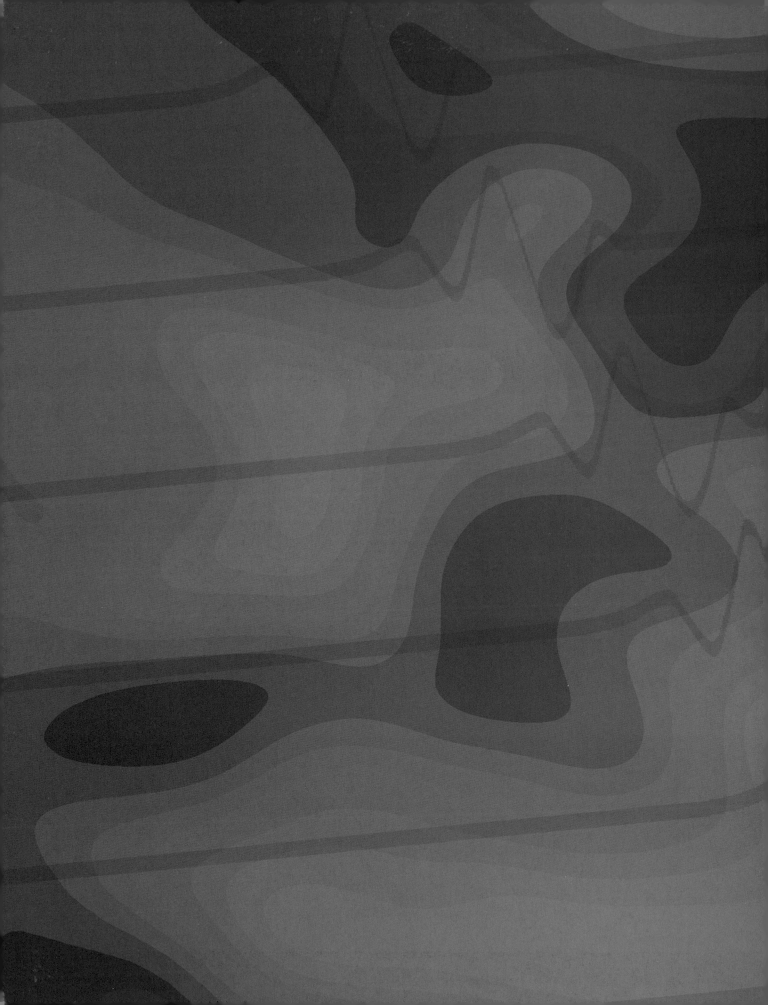